Animal Young

Insects

Rod Theodorou

P

Heinemann
LIBRARY

www.heinemann.co.uk
Visit our website to find out more information about **Heinemann Library** books.

To order:
☎ Phone 44 (0) 1865 888066
▤ Send a fax to 44 (0) 1865 314091
▯ Visit the Heinemann Bookshop at www.heinemann.co.uk to browse our catalogue and order online.

First published in Great Britain by
Heinemann Library,
Halley Court, Jordan Hill, Oxford OX2 8EJ
a division of Reed Educational and Professional
Publishing Ltd.
Heinemann is a registered trademark of Reed
Educational & Professional Publishing Ltd.

OXFORD MELBOURNE AUCKLAND
JOHANNESBURG BLANTYRE GABORONE
IBADAN PORTSMOUTH (NH) USA CHICAGO

Designed by Celia Floyd
Illustrations by Alan Fraser
Printed in Hong Kong/China

ISBN 0 431 03076 6 (hardback)
04 03 02 01 00
10 9 8 7 6 5 4 3 2

ISBN 0 431 03077 4 (paperback)
04 03 02 01 00
10 9 8 7 6 5 4 3 2 1

British Library Cataloguing in Publication Data

Theodorou, Rod
  Insects. – (Animal young)
  1. Insects – Infancy – Juvenile literature
  I. Title
  597.7'139

Acknowledgements
The Publishers would like to thank the following for
permission to reproduce photographs:

BBC: Hans Christoph Kappel p. 6, Pete Oxford p. 9;
Bruce Coleman: Kim Taylor p. 8, Felix Labhardt;
Frank Lane: E & D Hosking p. 8, B Borrell p. 13;
NHPA: Martin Harvey p. 7, Anthony Bannister p. 22,
Stephen Dalton pp. 17, 18, 24; Oxford Scientific
Films: Phil Devries p. 5, Tim Shepherd p. 10, Scott
Camazine p. 11, Avril Ramage p. 12, J H Robinson, p.
15, K G Vock p. 16, G I Bernard p. 19, P & W Ward
pp. 20, 21, Neil Bromhall, p. 23; Tony Stone: Art
Wolfe p. 14.

Cover photograph reproduced with permission of
Oxford Scientific Films/Michael Fogden

Every effort has been made to contact copyright
holders of any material reproduced in this book.
Any omissions will be rectified in subsequent
printings if notice is given to the Publisher.

Any words appearing in the text in bold, **like this**,
are explained in the Glossary.

Contents

Introduction

There are many different kinds of animals. All animals have babies. They look after their babies in different ways.

These are the six main animal groups.

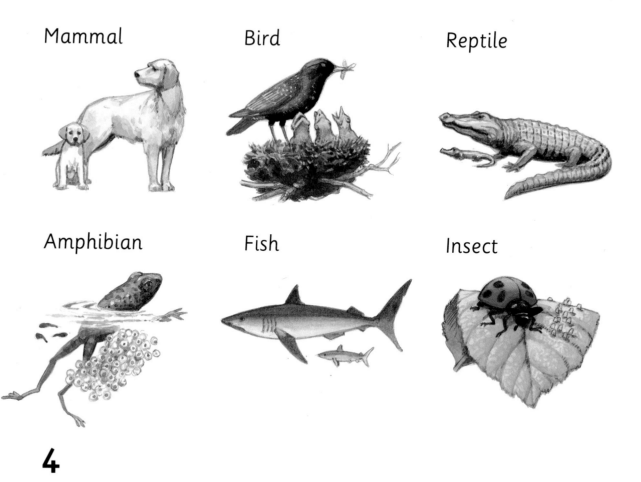

Mammal   Bird   Reptile

Amphibian   Fish   Insect

This book is about insects. There are more insects in the world than any other kind of animal. Most lay eggs. The young often look very different to their parents.

This is an adult fungus beetle next to its young.

what is an insect?

All adult insects:
- have three parts to their bodies
- have six legs
- have two feelers called antennae.

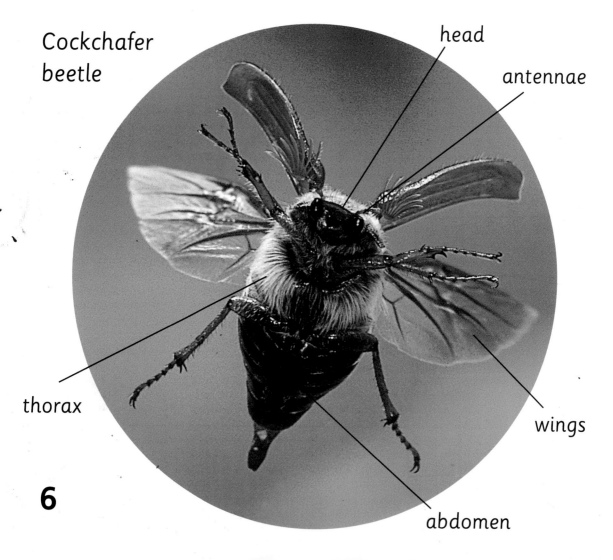

Cockchafer beetle

head

antennae

thorax

wings

abdomen

6

Most insects:

- have two or four wings to help them fly
- lay eggs that **hatch** into babies.

When this Giant Atlas Silk Moth is at rest
it leaves its four wings open.

Most insects lay their eggs near a plant or a dead animal so that when their young **hatch** they will have something to eat.

Baby flies are called **maggots**.

Some wasps sting a caterpillar or beetle and put it into a hole. They lay an egg in this hole, so their young will have something to eat when it hatches.

This sand wasp is dragging a caterpillar to its **burrow** for its young to eat.

Looking after the eggs

Most insects do not look after their eggs. Once they have laid them they just fly away. A few insects do stay with their eggs and young, **protecting** them from **enemies**.

This female earwig looks after her eggs.

Some insects like ants, termites, and some bees and wasps are different. Thousands of them live together in a **colony**. They take very good care of their eggs and young.

Worker bees look after the **queen** bee's eggs.

Hatching eggs

When the eggs **hatch**, some kinds of insect young look very different to their parents. These are called **larvae**. Many larvae eat their old egg cases.

These ladybird larvae do not look like their parents.

12

Other kinds of insect young look more like their parents. These are called **nymphs**. The nymphs do not have wings. Some live under water.

This dragonfly nymph hatches and lives under water.

Finding food

Nymphs and **larvae** are always hungry! Some eat huge amounts of leaves and fruit.

The larvae of butterflies and moths are called caterpillars.

Other young insects attack and eat other animals.
Many eat other insects.

This ant lion larvae digs a hole in the
sand and waits to attack passing ants
that fall in.

Looking after the young

Most insects do not take care of their young. They may even eat them! Insects that live in **colonies** do look after their eggs and **larvae**.

These ants look after their young in underground nests.

Insects that live in colonies often have a special room they keep their eggs and young in. They bring their young food to eat.

Worker honeybees bring their **grubs** food to eat.

Staying hidden

Many animals feed on young insects. Some young insects try to stay hidden from their **enemies**. They are often the same colour as the plants they live on.

These Kentish glory moth caterpillars stay hidden by being the same colour as the leaves they eat.

Some **nymphs** that live in water need to hide from hungry fish. They make a home out of bits of plant and sand. They carry their homes around with them.

This caddis fly nymph is hard to spot.

Keep away!

Some insects have a horrible taste. They have very brightly coloured skin that warns **predators** they taste bad.

Cinnabar moth caterpillars taste horrible.

Another way insects stop being eaten is to surprise their **enemies**. Some insects try to make themselves look like a bigger animal to scare their enemies.

The black dots on this puss moth caterpillar look like big scary eyes.

Amazing changes

As insect **larvae** grow they get too big for their skin. Their skin splits and they climb out, with bigger skin. This is called **shedding**.

This ladybird larva is shedding its skin.

The skin splits for the last time leaving a **pupa**. Inside the pupa the larva is changing. Soon it splits open and the adult insect comes out.

This ladybird is crawling out of its pupa.

Splitting skins

Nymphs do not turn into **pupa**. They already look a lot like an adult insect. When they are big enough they split their skins for the very last time.

This dragonfly nymph has climbed out of the water and is ready to **shed** its skin.

This adult dragonfly is climbing out of its nymph skin. Its wings look very crumpled but will soon grow big and strong.

The adult insects climb out of the nymph skin. The new adult insect often stays very still while blood pumps around its new body.

Growing up

This is how an insect **larva** grows up. The larva does not look like its parents.

Growth of a swallowtail butterfly

1 The adult female lays her eggs.

2 The larvae **hatch** from the eggs. Butterfly larvae are called caterpillars.

3 The caterpillars eat lots of food. They get bigger and bigger.

4 The caterpillar turns into a **pupa**.

5 A new adult butterfly crawls out of the pupa.

This is how an insect **nymph** grows up. The nymph looks a lot like its parents.

Growth of a grasshopper

1 The adult female lays her eggs in a hole in the sand.

2 The tiny nymphs hatch from the eggs.

3 The nymphs eat all day. Soon they split their skins.

4 Each time they split their skins they get bigger.

5 The nymph splits its skin for the last time and becomes an adult.

27

Insects and other animals

		Fish
What they look like:	Bones inside body	all
	Number of legs	none
	Hair on body	none
	Scaly skin	most
	Wings	none
	Feathers	none
Where they live:	Lives on land	none
	Lives in water	all
How they are born:	Grows babies inside body	some
	Lays eggs	most
How they feed young:	Feeds baby milk	none
	Bring babies food	none

	Amphibians	Insects	Reptiles	Birds	Mammals
	all	none	all	all	all
	4 or none	6	4 or none	2	2 or 4
	none	all	none	none	all
	none	none	all	none	few
	none	most	none	all	some
	none	none	none	all	none
	most	most	most	all	most
	some	some	some	none	some
	few	some	some	none	most
	most	most	most	all	few
	none	none	none	none	all
	none	some	none	most	most

Glossary

burrow   a hole that an animal makes in the ground to live or hide eggs in

colony   a group of insects that live together

enemy   an animal that will kill another animal for food or for its home

grub   a type of larva

hatch   to be born from an egg

larva   (more than one = larvae) animal baby that hatches from an egg but looks different to an adult

maggot   a baby fly

nymph   a young insect that looks very like an adult insect when it is born

predator   an animal that hunts and kills other animals for food

protect   to look after

pupa   a shell of skin that a larva grows inside

queen   mother insect

shed   to lose an old layer of skin when a new, bigger one has grown

workers   ants that do all the work in a colony, like building tunnels and feeding the young

Further reading

Ant, Karen Hartley and Chris Macro, *Bug Books*, Heinemann Library, 1998

Bee, Karen Hartley and Chris Macro, *Bug Books*, Heinemann Library, 1998

Big and Small, Rod Theodorou and Carole Telford, *Spot the Difference*, Heinemann Library, 1996.

Butterflies and Insects, Paul Sterry, *Tracker Nature Guides*, Hamlyn, 1991.

Caterpillar, Karen Hartley, Chris Macro and Philip Taylor, *Bug Books*, Heinemann Library, 1998

Cockroach, Karen Hartley, Chris Macro and Philip Taylor, *Bug Books*, Heinemann Library, 1998

Grasshopper, Karen Hartley, Chris Macro and Philip Taylor, *Bug Books*, Heinemann Library, 1998

Ladybird, Karen Hartley and Chris Macro, *Bug Books*, Heinemann Library, 1998

Mosquito, Karen Hartley and Chris Macro, *Bug Books*, Heinemann Library, 1998

Stick Insect, Karen Hartley, Chris Macro and Philip Taylor, *Bug Books*, Heinemann Library, 1998

Termite, Karen Hartley, Chris Macro and Philip Taylor, *Bug Books*, Heinemann Library, 1998

Through a Termite City, Rod Theodorou and Carole Telford, *Amazing Journeys*, Heinemann Library, 1997.

Index